Cooking

Kay Robertson

Rourke
Educational Media

rourkeeducationalmedia.com

www.rourkeeducationalmedia.com

PHOTO CREDITS: Cover: © Willie B. Thomas, © hatman12; page 2: © AshleyPickering; page 4: © fotomy; page 5: © burwellphotography; page 6: © nicolamargaret; page 7: © CharlotteLake; page 9: © Christopher Elwell; page 11: © KevinDyer; page 12: © leonkenig; page 14: © Vlue, © Peng Li, © nitrub, © trubach; page 15: © KathyDewar; page 17: © Ericlefrancais; page 18: © jkbowers; page 19: © piotr_malczyk; page 21: © MarkCoffeyPhoto; page 22: © Zaretska Olga; page 23: © kingvald; page 24: © JazzIRT; page 25: © DRB Images, LLC; page 26: © Rich Legg; page 27: © JoeDphoto; page 28: © FocusEye; page 29: © jorender; page 30: © jamirae; page 31: © aydinmutlu; page 32: © Carolyn Franks; page 33: © skodonnell; page 34: © jmbatt; page 35: © ebstock; page 36: © skhoward; page 37: © RichVintage; pages 38-39: © KathyDewar; page 40: © Moncherie; page 41: © PhotoTalk; page 42: © gojak; page 43: © Jani Bryson; page 44: © aylinstock; back cover

Editor: Jill Sherman

Cover design by Nicola Stratford

Interior design by Tara Raymo

Library of Congress PCN Data

STEM Guides to Cooking / Kay Robertson.
    p. cm. -- (STEM Everyday)
Includes index.
 ISBN 978-1-62169-851-7 (hardcover)
 ISBN 978-1-62169-746-6 (softcover)
 ISBN 978-1-62169-954-5 (e-Book)
Library of Congress Control Number: 2013936457

Also Available as:

ROURKE'S
e-Books

Rourke Educational Media
Printed in the United States of America,
North Mankato, Minnesota

Rourke

rourkeeducationalmedia.com
customerservice@rourkeeducationalmedia.com • PO Box 643328 Vero Beach, Florida 32964

Table of Contents

Introduction

People use math to work with food in all sorts of ways. When your parents buy food they use math to figure out exactly how much it will cost.

You can use simple math to help your parents know how long the food in the refrigerator will keep fresh. Simple math will also help you find out how much food you have eaten.

When your parents buy food, they use math to find out how much the food will cost. If these ears of corn are 50 cents each, how much will five ears cost?

On the other hand, the math becomes very complex after you've eaten food. When food enters your body it travels to the stomach to be digested, or converted to energy. Math can give you an idea of how much energy you can expect to get out of a particular food!

Stomach

The stomach is where food is digested, or broken down for use as fuel.

Recipes

Have you ever made a peanut butter and jelly sandwich? How did you do it?

How would you explain to someone else how to make a peanut butter and jelly sandwich?

You would probably say something like:

1) Get two slices of bread, peanut butter, and jelly.

2) Spread some peanut butter on one slice of bread, and some jelly on the other slice of bread.

3) Put the two pieces of bread together, with the spreads on the inside, to make a sandwich.

Recipes are very much like mathematical formulas.

That's a **recipe**, a set of instructions telling someone how to make something. The bread, peanut butter, and jelly are all **ingredients** in the recipe.

The instructions, or recipe, for making a peanut butter and jelly sandwich are very simple. Recipes can be simple or complex, but they always follow the same pattern. They give a set of ingredients and tell you what to do with them to create the finished product.

Foods like brownies, lasagna, or soup are made with more complicated recipes. They are complicated because they use many different ingredients and require very specific amounts of each. Determining an exact amount of something is called **measuring**. Let's take a look at the ingredients in a complex recipe. Here are the ingredients in a recipe for chocolate brownies:

1/2 cup butter

1 cup white sugar

2 eggs

1 teaspoon vanilla extract

1/3 cup unsweetened cocoa powder

1/2 cup all-purpose flour

1/4 teaspoon salt

1/4 teaspoon baking powder

You can probably see the difference between this recipe and the recipe for the peanut butter and jelly sandwich. This recipe doesn't just say some eggs, it calls for two eggs. You're dealing with exact amounts.

You have probably noticed that recipes uses terms like cup or tablespoon. These are **units of measure**. Cups and tablespoons are units of measure typically used in cooking.

These measurements are useful because they make altering recipes very simple. For example, this brownie recipe makes 16 brownies. What if you wanted to make twice that amount? All you would have to do is multiply the amounts of the ingredients by two.

Multiplication is a way of adding large groups of numbers.

STEM in Action?

You have a recipe that makes 16 brownies. What would twice that amount be? You can find out in a couple of different ways. You can add 16 and 16. Or, you can use multiplication to get the same result.

$$16 + 16 = 32$$
$$2 \times 16 = 32$$

In a multiplication equation, each number has a particular name. In this case, the number 2 is called the multiplicand. The number of brownies, 16, is the multiplier.

The answer to your question is the product. By doubling the ingredients in this recipe, you can make 32 brownies.

When doubling the ingredients, you may want to convert the measurements expressed in fractions into decimal numbers. This is easy to do, since a fraction is really just another way of expressing a **division** problem.

STEM Fast Fact!

Small Amounts

Some of the numbers in the converted brownie recipe might seem a little strange to you. For instance, how would you measure .66 cup unsweetened cocoa powder? Just remember that half a cup would be .5, so .66 is a little more than that, or 2/3 of a cup. Sometimes a recipe will call for a very small amount of an ingredient. You might see terms like a dash of pepper or a pinch of salt. These terms indicate quantities that are too small for measure. Rather than specifying a ridiculously small amount, .000125 of a tablespoon, the amount to be added is left up to the cook.

STEM in Action?

The first item in the brownie recipe, 1/2 cup butter, can also be expressed as a division equation:

$$1 \div 2 = .5$$

The numbers in a division equation also have names: 1 is the dividend, 2 is the divisor, and the answer, .5, is called the quotient.

Now convert all the fractions in the recipe:

> 1/2 cup butter = .5 cup butter
>
> 1 cup white sugar = 1 cup white sugar
>
> 2 eggs = 2 eggs
>
> 1 teaspoon vanilla extract = 1 teaspoon vanilla extract
>
> 1/3 cup unsweetened cocoa powder = .33 cup unsweetened cocoa powder
>
> 1/2 cup all-purpose flour = .5 cup all-purpose flour
>
> 1/4 teaspoon salt = .25 teaspoon salt
>
> 1/4 teaspoon baking powder = .25 teaspoon baking powder

Now that you have converted your list of ingredients, you just have to multiply them by two:

> .5 cup butter x 2 = 1 cup butter
>
> 1 cup white sugar x 2 = 2 cups white sugar
>
> 2 eggs x 2 = 4 eggs
>
> 1 teaspoon vanilla extract x 2 = 2 teaspoons vanilla extract
>
> .33 cup unsweetened cocoa powder x 2 = .66 cup unsweetened cocoa powder
>
> .5 cup all-purpose flour x 2 = 1 cup all-purpose flour
>
> .25 teaspoon salt x 2 = .5 teaspoon salt
>
> .25 teaspoon baking powder x 2 = .5 teaspoon baking powder

Now you have a recipe for making 32 brownies!

Different Ways to Measure

When following a recipe, you use cooking measures, like tablespoons, cups, quarts, and gallons.

The standards for cooking measure apply to both dry ingredients like flour and liquid quantities like milk. If you were making something that called for 1 cup of flour and 1 cup of milk, you could use the same cup to measure both ingredients.

However, if you look at these items in a supermarket, you'll see that they are measured in different ways. The items in a supermarket are usually divided into dry quantities and liquid quantities. Dry quantities include things like rice, flour, or cereal, while liquid quantities include milk, soda, and orange juice. A container of milk isn't measured in cups, it is measured in gallons. Likewise, a bag of flour isn't measured in cups, it is measured in pounds.

Part of the reason for this difference is that cups are a relatively small amount. If all the items in a supermarket were measured in cups, there would be some very large numbers on the food labels.

Cup   Pint   Quart   Gallon

Liquid quantities are measured according to liquid volume or capacity.

Units of Measure for Liquid	
1 tablespoon	3 teaspoons
1 tablespoon	0.5 fluid ounces
1 cup	8 fluid ounces
1 pint	2 cups
1 quart	2 pints
1 gallon	4 quarts
1 bushel	8 gallons

STEM in Action?

Using the chart, you can determine how many cups are in a half-gallon container of milk.

1 cup = 8 fluid ounces

1 pint = 2 cups

1 quart = 2 pints

1 gallon = 4 quarts

Working backward and using multiplication, you can determine how many cups are in 1 gallon:

1 gallon = 4 quarts

4 x (1 quart = 2 pints) gives 4 quarts = 8 pints

8 x (1 pint = 2 cups) gives 8 pints = 16 cups

So, if there are 16 cups to a gallon, you can find out the number of cups in a half-gallon by dividing this result by 2:

$$16 \div 2 = 8$$

A half-gallon container of milk contains 8 cups!

Dry quantities, on the other hand, are usually measured by **weight**. Dry quantities include items like butter, rice, and peanut butter.

STEM Fast Fact!

Take a look at the weight label from a standard jar of peanut butter. What does all that mean?

NET WT. 18 OZ.
(1 LB. 2 OZ.)

NET wt. can be read as net weight, and oz, is an abbreviation for ounces. So, reading the first line aloud, you would say that the jar of peanut butter's net weight is eighteen ounces.

Concentrate on the second line. lb. is the abbreviation for pound. This line, therefore, can be read as one pound, two ounces.

STEM in Action?

If the jar of peanut butter contains 18 ounces, and there are 16 ounces in a pound, then how many pounds of peanut butter are in the jar?

There are 18 ounces, so you know that the jar contains at least 1 pound of peanut butter. What's left?

$$18 - 16 = 2$$

2 ounces!

The jar of peanut butter contains one pound, 2 ounces of peanut butter!

How about a box of cereal that contains 21 ounces of cereal? How would you express that in pounds?

$$21 - 16 = 5$$

The box of cereal contains 1 pound, 5 ounces of cereal!

STEM Fast Fact!

Meats and Fish

Weight is also the system of measurement for foods such as ground beef, chicken, cold meats, and fish. If you have ever gone to a butcher's shop or visited a deli counter, you've probably heard people asking for "a half pound of turkey" or "a quarter pound of roast beef." These people are expressing fractions:

A half pound of turkey = 1/2 lb. of turkey

A quarter pound of roast beef = 1/4 lb. of roast beef

Meats and fish are always measured in pounds. If each of these fish weigh 1/2 pound, and they are priced at $7 per pound, how much would it cost to buy three fish?

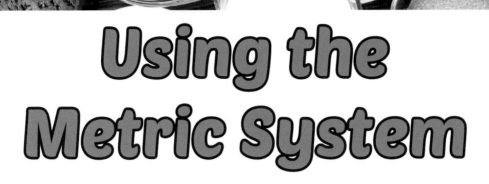

Using the Metric System

We actually have two systems of weights and measure in the United States. Quarts, pints, gallons, ounces, and pounds are all units of the U.S. Customary System, also known as the English System.

The other system of measurement, and the only one sanctioned by the United States Government, is the **metric system**, which is also known as the International System of Units.

Most of the world uses the metric system. If you were to do your shopping at a grocery store in Europe, for example, all of the dry quantities would be measured in grams, while the liquid quantities would be measured in liters. Meanwhile, the items in an American supermarket are actually measured in both systems.

STEM Fast Fact!

Here are the specifications for a tub of butter:

NET WT 1lb. (453 grams)

You know that this means the net weight of the tub of butter is 1 pound. But what about that other number, 453 grams?

Grams are a metric unit of dry measure. The tub of butter contains 1 pound of butter, which can also be measured as 453 grams of butter.

Here are the units for converting between the U.S. Customary System of Measure and the metric system:

Dry Measure	Liquid Measure
1 ounce = 28.3495 grams	1 cup = 0.236 liters
1 pound = 453.59 grams	1 pint = 0.473 liters
	1 quart = 0.946 liters
	1 gallon = 3.78 liters

Source: 2000 New York Times Almanac

Using this table, you can do some math to convert the quantities used in the United States to something people in the rest of the world can understand.

Try This

If you have two pounds of flour, how many grams is that equal to?

STEM in Action?

If a box of rice contains 7 ounces of rice, how many grams is that? You can find out by using multiplication. You know that 1 ounce is equal to 28.3 grams, so:

$$7 \times 28.3 = 198.1$$

7 ounces of is equal to 198 grams.

What about a half-gallon of milk? How much would that be expressed in liters? To figure this out, you can use division. You know that 1 gallon is equal to 3.78 liters. So if you divide 3.78 by 2:

$$3.78 \div 2 = 1.89$$

A half-gallon is 1.89 liters.

STEM Fast Fact!

The Creation of the Metric System

French scientists developed the metric system during the 1790s. The basic unit of measurement in the metric system is the meter, which is about one ten-millionth the distance from the North Pole to the equator.

Keep It Cold

Unfortunately, foods do not last forever. Your family has probably had to throw away food that has gone bad.

You cannot stop food from spoiling, but you can delay it from happening. There are a couple of different ways to do this, and they are both at work in your kitchen. What are they?

The refrigerator and freezer are the most useful tools we have for keeping foods fresh. Most refrigerators have an attached freezer compartment that can be kept colder than the main refrigerator compartment. The colder freezer is used for long-term storage. Some families even have a separate freezer where they can store larger quantities of foods.

Foods spoil because of **bacteria** growth. You can slow down this process by keeping foods in the refrigerator. The low temperature in the refrigerator slows the growth of bacteria.

The temperature inside of a refrigerator or freezer is much lower than room temperature, which is 72 degrees Fahrenheit (22 degrees Celsius). The recommended temperature for inside the refrigerator is 35 degrees Fahrenheit (2 degrees Celsius).

STEM in Action?

How much cooler is the temperature inside the refrigerator compared to room temperature? You can find out by using subtraction:

$$72 - 35 = 37$$

The temperature inside the refrigerator is 37 degrees lower than room temperature.

Now how about the temperature inside the freezer? The recommended temperature inside a freezer is 4 degrees Fahrenheit.

How much lower is the temperature inside the freezer compared to room temperature? Again, you can find out by using subtraction:

$$72 - 4 = 68$$

The temperature inside the freezer is 68 degrees lower than room temperature. That's pretty cold!

STEM Fast Fact!

Expiration Dates

All food has an **expiration date** listed somewhere on the package. This date gives you an idea of when a food will spoil. It is a good idea to pay attention to the expiration date, especially when eating foods that spoil quickly, such as milk or butter.

If it is the 16th of the month, and the tub of butter in your refrigerator has an expiration date of the 18th, how many more days is the butter still good?

$$18 - 16 = 2$$

The butter is good for two more days!

Cook It!

Certain kinds of bacteria can make you very sick. It is not something that you want in your food. This is why people refrigerate and freeze foods. It is also why people cook foods.

Refrigeration is a way of preventing the growth of bacteria by lowering the temperature. Cooking, meanwhile, is a way of killing bacteria that has already grown by raising the temperature.

While it is true that some foods can be safely eaten when uncooked, there are some cases where cooking food is necessary. This is the case with meats, poultry, and eggs.

The three methods of heat transfer are conduction, convection, and radiation. Conduction is the transfer of heat through solids. Convection, on the other hand, is the transfer of heat through fluids. Finally, radiation is the transfer of heat through space. Most methods of cooking fall into one of the first two categories. For instance, what if you wanted to cook some hot dogs? Frying the hot dogs in a pan on the stove would be cooking by conduction. If you filled the pan with water and boiled the hot dogs, that would be cooking by convection.

The kitchen stove is where people do most of their cooking. The burners on the stovetop are not marked with temperatures. Burners usually just have knobs indicating low, medium, and high settings.

STEM in Action **?**

What if a recipe for a cake told you to put the cake batter into the oven for 55 minutes at a temperature of 350 degrees Fahrenheit? How much higher would the temperature in the oven be compared to room temperature?

350 – 72 = 278

The temperature in an oven heated to 350 degrees is 278 degrees higher than room temperature. That's hot enough to kill any bacteria living in the food.

Cooking in the oven is much more specific. The knobs for the oven are very precise. Usually, they list temperatures in increments of 50, like 300, 350, 400, 450, and so on.

If the boiling point for water is 212 degrees Fahrenheit, how hot would you say the burner under this kettle is?

If the temperature in this oven is 450 degrees Fahrenheit, how much hotter is that compared to room temperature?

Food Labels

How many meals do you eat in a day? You probably eat three meals a day: breakfast, lunch, and dinner. But, have you ever skipped a meal? If so, what happened? You probably got hungry, but do you know why?

The answer is simple. Food is fuel for your body. Just like a car cannot run without fuel, your body cannot work without food. Hunger is your body's way of saying it needs more fuel.

We eat reguglarly in order to keep our bodies going. Food enables our bodies to grow, breathe, think, and repair tissue. Food provides us with the nourishment that we need to live.

Like gasoline for a car, food is your body's fuel. Can you think of different ways that you use that fuel?

Do you have a favorite food? Maybe you said broccoli. Maybe you said chocolate!

In a perfect world, broccoli and chocolate would have the same nutritional value. Unfortunately, this isn't the case. Some foods are just better for us than others.

This is where nutritional labels come in handy.

Food labels give us a summary of what is good and bad about a particular food. These labels are especially useful when you consider how much of what we eat is made of several different foods.

For instance, what goes into a pie? It is made of several different things, including sugar, flour, fruit, and many other ingredients. It is fairly simple to say how nutritious one of those ingredients is, but with the Nutrition Facts label you can see how nutritious all of those ingredients are in combination.

STEM Fast Fact!

A food label looks complicated, but it becomes a little easier if you break it down into sections.

A typical food label is made of three sections:

1) **Serving Size**
2) **Calories**
3) **Nutrients**

Nutrition Facts on food labels contain all the information you need to make decisions for healthy eating.

Nutrition Facts
Serving Size 1 cup (240mL)
Servings Per Container about 2

Amount Per Serving	
Calories 150 Calories from Fat 25	
	% Daily Value*
Total Fat 2.5g	4%
Saturated Fat 1.5g	8%
Cholesterol 10mg	3%
Sodium 960mg	40%
Total Carbohydrate 24g	8%
Dietary Fiber 2g	8%
Sugars 5g	
Protein 9g	

Vitamin A 70%	•	Vitamin C 0%
Calcium 2%	•	Iron 6%

* Percent Daily Values are based on a 2,000 calorie diet. Your daily values may be higher or lower depending on your calorie needs:

		Calories:	2,000	2,500
Total Fat	Less than		65g	80g
Sat Fat	Less than		20g	25g
Cholesterol	Less than		300mg	300mg
Sodium	Less than		2,400mg	2,400mg
Total Carbohydrate			300g	375g
Dietary Fiber			25g	30g

CONDENSED

PARIS INTERNATIONAL EXPOSITION 1900

Chicken Noodle SOUP

NET WT
10 ¾ OZ
(305

The first section, the serving size, should seem familiar to you. That is because it is based on cooking measurements.

In this case, the can of soup, the serving size reads:
Serving Size 1 cup (240 milliliters)
Servings Per Container about 2

So there are two cups of soup in the can. It is important to understand this, because all the numbers that follow are all based on the serving size of one cup. In other words, if you ate the entire can of soup, you would be getting twice the amount of **calories**, sodium, and cholesterol listed.

STEM in Action?

Let's focus on what the nutrition label says for sugar:

Sugars 5g

So one serving (1 cup of soup) contains 5 grams of sugar. But how much sugar would you be getting if you ate the entire can?

5 grams x 2 = 10 grams

If you ate the whole can of soup, you would get 10 grams of sugar!

Counting Calories

You may have heard of people counting calories in order to lose weight. But what are calories?

Strictly speaking, a calorie is a measurement of heat energy. Remember the metric system? A calorie is the amount of heat needed to raise the temperature of 1 gram of pure water 1 degree centigrade.

The body stores excess calories as fat, which is how people gain weight.

Foods that are high in calories contain a lot of potential energy. But if you don't use that energy, the body stores it as fat and you gain weight.

Monitoring calorie intake is important in monitoring a healthy body weight. That is why calories are listed at the top of a nutrition label.

Calories from fat is another number people pay attention to if they are trying to lose weight.

STEM in Action?

The calories section of a label looks like this:

Calories 150   Calories from Fat 25

In this case, what percentage of the can of soup is fat?

You can find out by using division. First divide 25 by 150:

$$25 \div 150 = .16$$

Then, multiply the result by 100 to express it as a percentage:

$$.16 \times 100 = 16$$

So, 16 percent of the calories are from fat.

37

Exercise is a great way to burn calories and stay healthy. The important thing is to find a type of exercise that you enjoy.

STEM Fast Fact!

The 2,000 Calorie Diet

The amount of calories a person should eat in a day depends on a lot of different factors. These include the person's overall health, including his or her present weight, the type of work he or she does, and the amount of exercise he or she gets. People who work in manual labor or exercise on a regular basis need more calories than people who don't. But, for the most part, 2,000 calories is about what the average adult should consume in a single day. That is what is meant by a 2,000 calorie diet.

Using that measure, if you ate 1 cup of soup at 150 calories, how many calories would you have left for the day?

$$2,000 - 150 = 1,850$$

1,850 calories!

Nutrition Knowledge

The nutrition label also contains information about **nutrients**. Nutrients are the components of food, or what food is made of. In a sense, food is a container for nutrients. In the same way that you buy a can of soup for the food inside, you eat a food to give your body the nutrients inside of the soup.

Nutrition Facts

Serv Size 2 tbsp.(37g)
Servings about 20
Calories 200
  Fat Cal 100

*Percent Daily Values (DV) are based on a 2.000 calorie diet.

Amount/Serving	%DV*	Amount/Serving	%DV*
Total Fat 11g	**17%**	**Total Carb.** 22g	7%
Sat. Fat 3.5g	**18%**	Fiber 1g	6%
Trans Fat 0g		Sugars 21g	
Cholest. 0mg	**0%**	**Protein** 3g	
Sodium 15mg	**1%**		

Vitamin A 0% • Vitamin C 0% • Calcium 4% • Iron 4%

An **example** of a tasty yet balanced **breakfast:**

a glass of skim milk, orange juice and Nutella®

INGREDIENTS: SUGAR, MODIFIED PALM OIL, HAZELN... COCOA, SKIM MILK, REDUCED MINERALS WHEY (FR MILK), SOY LECITHIN: AN EMULSIFIER, VANILL... ARTIFICIAL FLAVOR.

MADE IN CANADA.

EXCL. DIST.FERRERO U.S.A, INC.

Look again at the label. Find the nutrients section, and you'll notice right away that there is a lot of math here. To the right of each of the different nutrients are percentages.

You've also probably noticed that this section of the food label is divided in half. On the top are nutrients like total fat, cholesterol, and sodium, while on the bottom are nutrients like vitamin A, vitamin C, and iron.

As with calories, the percentages listed for these nutrients are based on the 2,000 calorie diet. In the previous section we only talked about this reference in terms of calories, but now look at what it says regarding nutrients:

Total Fat – 11 g
Sat (Saturated) Fat – 3.5 g
Cholesterol – 0 mg
Sodium – 15 mg
Total Carbohydrates – 22 g
Dietary Fiber – 1 g

STEM in Action?

If a can of soup contains 2.5 grams of fat. What percentage of your daily allowance of fat would this be, based on the 2,000 calorie diet?

The 2,000 calorie diet recommends less than 65 grams of fat a day. The first step, then, is to divide the 2.5 grams of fat in the soup by 65.

$$2.5 \div 65 = 0.038$$

Next, multiply this number by 100 in order to change it to a percentage:

$$0.038 \times 100 = 3.8$$

Finally, round up that result to the nearest whole number:

$$4$$

So one serving of soup would contain about 4 percent of your total daily allowance of fat.

Here's a hint. You can check the soup can label to see if your math is correct.

Scientists disagree about what a healthy amount of sugar is. Although it provides quick energy, sugar is probably healthiest in small amounts.

Conclusion

The next time you step into your kitchen, you will see it in a brand new way. This is because you now know how much math is going on in that room! From refrigeration to cooking, food has a lot more to do with math than you may have ever realized.

How about the supermarket? The next time you go there look at all the different food labels. Maybe you can even teach someone else how to read them!

Now that you really understand measuring, maybe you'll try to do more cooking. Since you now know how to alter food recipes, you can cook for as many or as few people as necessary!

Glossary

bacteria (bak-TIHR-ee-uh): very small organisms that can grow in food and cause people to become sick

calories (KAL-uh-ree): the amount of heat needed to raise the temperature of 1 gram of pure water 1 degree centigrade

expiration date (ek-spe-RA-shen DAYT): the date at which a food spoils

ingredients (in-GREE-dee-uhntz): different foods used in a recipe

measuring (MEZH-ur-ing): determining an exact amount of something

metric system (MET-rik SISS-tuhm): the standard of measurement used by most of the world

nutrients (NOO-tree-uhntz): elements contained in food that enable the body to carry out its essential functions

recipe (RESS-i-pee): a group of instructions that explain how to make something

units of measure (YOO-nitz UHV MEZH-ur): set quantities for either dry or liquid goods such as cup, tablespoon, pound, and ounce

weight (WATE): a measure of how heavy something is

Index

Metric System

In the United States, we typically measure cooking ingredients by volume. But most of the world measures these ingredients by weight, using the metric system.

You can use the chart below to convert recipes for use in other countries.

Volume Conversions: Normally Used for Liquids Only	
Customary quantity	Metric equivalent
1 teaspoon	5 milliliters
1 tablespoon or 1/2 fluid ounce	15 milliliters
1 fluid ounce or 1/8 cup	30 milliliters
1/4 cup or 2 fluid ounces	60 milliliters
1/3 cup	80 milliliters
1/2 cup or 4 fluid ounces	120 milliliters
2/3 cup	160 milliliters
3/4 cup or 6 fluid ounces	180 milliliters
1 cup or 8 fluid ounces or half a pint	240 milliliters
1 1/2 cups or 12 fluid ounces	350 milliliters
2 cups or 1 pint or 16 fluid ounces	475 milliliters
3 cups or 1 1/2 pints	700 milliliters
4 cups or 2 pints or 1 quart	950 milliliters
4 quarts or 1 gallon	3.8 liters

Note: In cases where higher precision is not justified, it may be convenient to round these conversions off as follows:
  1 cup = 250 millileters
  1 pint = 500 millileters
  1 quart = 1 liter
  1 gallon = 4 liters

Websites to Visit

www.howstuffworks.com/food.htm

www.wcsscience.com/room/temperature.html

vm.cfsan.fda.gov/label.html

www.howstuffworks.com/question670.htm

www.infoplease.com/ipa/A0001661.html

Show What You Know

1. How would you double a recipe?

2. What units are used to measure liquids?

3. What are ingredients?

4. At what temperature should you keep your refrigerator?

5. Where would you look to find the serving size of a can of soup?